Living Thoughts
for the
Children's
Hour

Books by Kenneth N. Taylor:
  The Bible in Pictures for Little Eyes
  The New Testament in Pictures for Little Eyes
  Devotions for the Children's Hour
  Stories for the Children's Hour
  The Living Bible (Tyndale House Publishers)

LIVING THOUGHTS
for the
CHILDREN'S HOUR

by

Kenneth N. Taylor

MOODY PRESS
CHICAGO

Original title: *I See*

2 3 4 5 6 7 8 Printing/LC/Year 95 94 93 92 91 90

ISBN: 0-8024-2228-4

Printed in the United States of America

Contents

1

Heaven

Do you know where heaven is? Heaven is a place somewhere far away in the sky where Jesus and the angels live. It is a beautiful place, more beautiful than we have ever seen before. Heaven is God's home, and so everything there is bright and beautiful, and no one is ever sick or sad.

Would you like to go there someday and see such a wonderful place? Lots of other boys and girls who are Jesus' friends are there, and they are very, very happy. Yes, I am sure you would like to go there too, and I will tell you how.

This little boy and girl in the picture want to go to heaven. They are looking up into the sky. They are trying to see the road that goes there. But soon they will find out something nice, and I will tell you what it is. They don't need a road or a street to get to heaven. Isn't that strange? There is no road to heaven. But someday Jesus will come and get us if we want Him to, and He will take us there right through the sky.

Everybody who loves Jesus can get to heaven that way. They can live there always in that beautiful place where everyone is happy and good.

A Story

A little boy and a little girl were walking along one day looking for the road to heaven. They loved Jesus and wanted to see Him and be near Him because He loves little children. They saw a nice man and woman and ran over to them. The little boy said, "Can you please tell us how to get to heaven? We can't find the road that goes up into the sky."

The man looked surprised and said, "Little boy, you can't get to heaven by walking or riding. You have to wait until Jesus comes to get you, and then you can go right up into the sky with Him."

"When will Jesus come to get us?" the little girl wanted to know.

"Jesus hasn't told us that," the man and woman said. "So you run home now and help your mother and do kind things that will make Jesus glad."

And that is just what the girl and the boy did.

Questions:

1. What are the little boy and the little girl in the picture trying to find?
2. Is there a street that goes up into the sky?
3. How can people get to heaven?

A prayer:

Dear Jesus, thank You for the nice home You are making for me up there in heaven. Help me to love You and do the things You want me to. In Your name. Amen.

A Bible thought:

Jesus said, I am going away to make a home for you in heaven, and then I will come back and get you so that you can live there with Me always (John 14:2).

Bible Reading: John 14:1-6

2

The Angels

Have you ever seen an angel? No, not very many people have, because when the angels walk around, nobody can see them unless the angels want them to. Probably some of them are right here with us in this room, but we can't see or feel them. Wouldn't it be fun to be an angel?

But God doesn't want you to be an angel, because He wants you to be His child. God wants you to be in His family. Even though to be an angel would be fun, it is far better for you to be God's child.

What do the angels do? They are God's helpers, and they help God's children. They help you and me. One of their jobs is to keep us from getting hurt, as in the picture. Do you see the angel taking care of the little boy and girl? They can't see the angel, but the angel is keeping them from falling. If one of the children slips, perhaps the angel will push him back again. That is what angels do sometimes.

Wherever God's little children go, angels are there to help them. Shall we thank God because we can be His children and have angels to help us?

A Story

This is a Bible story about the way God sent His angels to take care of two of His friends.

Elisha was the name of a good man who did whatever God told him to. Many people didn't like Elisha because God told Elisha to tell them they were bad. The people didn't like that, so they came to catch Elisha and hurt him.

Just then Elisha looked up and saw God's angels coming to help him. Elisha could see them, but no one else knew they were there. Even Elisha's friend who was standing there with him couldn't see them at first, so Elisha asked God to fix his friend's eyes so that he could see the angels too. God did this, and then both of them saw the angels. The angels helped them and took care of them.

Questions:

1. Are there any angels here in this room?
2. Can we always see the angels? Can they see us?
3. Who sends the angels to help us?
4. Do angels always keep us from getting hurt?

A prayer:

Our Father in heaven, thank You for Your angels that You send to help us. We want to be Your helpers too. Thank You for being so kind to us. In Jesus' name we pray. Amen.

A Bible thought:

He sends His angels to be our helpers (Hebrews 1:7).

Bible Reading: 2 Kings 6:8-17

3

You May Talk with the King!

Just suppose that you could go any time you wanted to and talk to a great king who would gladly give you anything you needed!

That would be very exciting and wonderful. But it would be ever so much more wonderful if you received an invitation from the great God of heaven to come and talk to Him. You would be so excited. You would think and talk about it and get ready very carefully to talk with God. For God, you remember, made the earth and people and the stars in the heavens and everything. He can do anything He wants to, and He loves you dearly.

Do you realize that God *has* invited you to come and talk with Him? He is even disappointed if you don't. He *wants* you to ask Him for things you need. He *loves* to give you things. He *enjoys* having you talk with Him.

Think of it! God, who is so holy and pure, is willing to talk to you. He will not command you to be punished for bothering Him. He loves you and wants you to come.

Do you see what this girl in the picture is doing? She's talking to God! God in heaven is listening to this girl while she talks to Him. Would you like to talk to Him too? You can if you are a friend of Jesus. God lets friends of Jesus come and talk to Him whenever they want to.

You can pray at night when you go to bed, in the daytime when walking to school, when you get home, and many other times. God is always glad to talk with you. Isn't that wonderful?

A Story

This is a true story of something that happened long ago. Some little children and their mothers were out walking one day. They saw Jesus talking to some men who were Jesus' friends. The children wanted to talk to Jesus because He was their Friend too. The mothers took the children by the hand, and together they went to talk to Jesus.

But when the men saw them coming, they looked angry. "Go away," they said. "Don't bother Jesus. He is too important to talk to children. Mothers, take those children away."

I think the children cried, don't you? They wanted to talk to Jesus, and the men wouldn't let them.

But then a wonderful thing happened. Jesus saw that the men were sending the children away.

"Oh, don't do that," He said. "Let the little children come to Me. I want to talk to them."

So the men stepped back and let the children come. Jesus took them on His lap and talked to them. Oh, they were happy then!

Would you like to come and talk to Jesus?

He wants you to, and He won't let anyone shoo you away.

Questions:

1. Where does Jesus live?
2. Can He hear you when you talk to Him?
3. Does Jesus like you to talk to Him?
4. Can you talk to Jesus even if you can't see Him?

A prayer:

Dear Lord Jesus, thank You for letting us come and talk to You even though You are so great and we are so small. Please help me to love You as I should and to come often to You, just as we are doing now. In Your name. Amen.

A Bible thought:

Jesus said, Let the little children come to Me (Matthew 19:14).

Bible Reading: Luke 18:15-17

4

Who Made Everything?

This little girl is talking to the man on the big tractor. A tractor is like an automobile, but it goes through fields on its big wheels and pulls heavy things after it. This man is using the tractor to pull a big plow that breaks up the ground. Then he will put seeds in the soft, warm earth, and soon green leaves of corn or wheat will come up.

The big tractor can help put the little seeds in the ground, but it cannot make the seeds grow. Only God can do that. God can do it because He is so great. God makes seeds and flowers, and He made the rocks and the sky. He made the sun and the moon and all the stars. And God made you.

You and I cannot make stars. We can make little things with a saw or a hammer, but only God can make stars and things like that. God is so great that He can do whatever He wants to, no matter what.

And always, always remember this: God loves you very, very much. He loves you, and gave Himself to die for you.

A Story

Billy and Alice were all excited about something. They had been outside playing, and they saw a pretty red flower.

"Oh, look," Alice said. "What a pretty flower! I wish there were two flowers instead of one."

"Well, let's make another," Billy said. "Then we'll have two."

"You can't make flowers," Alice told him. "They just have to grow. You put a seed in the ground, and it grows up and becomes a pretty flower."

"Well, then, let's make a seed," Billy said.

So that is why Billy and Alice were so excited. They ran into the house and got flour from Mother and put just a little water with it until they could make little white balls by rolling it between their fingers.

"See our seeds," they said to Mother. "Aren't they pretty?"

Then they colored the little balls red and black with their paint set and took them outdoors and put them in the soft ground.

"Now we'll have a red flower and a black flower," Billy said. "Pretty soon our seed will grow, and we will have some pretty flowers."

But Alice didn't think so.

Who do you think was right?

Questions:

1. Can people make seeds that will grow?
2. Who can?
3. Who can make stars?
4. Who made you?

A prayer:

O God, our heavenly Father, thank You for being so great and so good. Thank You for making me and for loving me. Please help me to love You and to do the things You like me to. In Jesus' name. Amen.

A Bible thought:

All things were made by Him (John 1:3).

Bible Reading: Genesis 1:1-8

5

Jesus Loves You

These children are looking at a picture and singing a song. Do you know whom they are looking at in the picture? Yes, it is a picture of Jesus with some children. Jesus loves children, and their fathers and mothers too. He wants them to come to Him so He can help them and talk to them. I will tell you what song the children are singing as they look at the picture. They are singing:

Jesus loves me, this I know
For the Bible tells me so;
Little ones to Him belong;
They are weak, but He is strong.
Yes, Jesus loves me,
Yes, Jesus loves me,
Yes, Jesus loves me,
The Bible tells me so.

Do you know that Jesus loves you just as He loves the children in the picture? He wants to talk to you and help you. He wants to be your Friend always and always and always. No one but Jesus can take you up to heaven when you die. Only Jesus' friends can be in heaven with Him because that is what God says. Are you a friend of Jesus? Are you willing to do whatever He tells you to? Can you decide right now that whatever Jesus tells you, you will do? Then you will be Jesus' friend, and He will be your Friend forever.

A Story

Carol was crying. Mother told her to put her dolls away, and she said no. So Mother had spanked her for not doing what she was told. That night after dinner when Mother had kissed her and tucked her into bed, Carol started crying again.

"Why, Carol!" Mother asked. "What is the matter?"

"I am sorry I said I wouldn't put my dolls away," Carol sobbed. "And now Jesus doesn't like me anymore."

"Oh," Mother said, "so that's it." And then Mother told Carol some wonderful news. "Jesus still loves you just as much," she said. "Jesus knew you were going to be bad this afternoon. He died on the cross for you so that God could forgive you. He took away the badness. That's how much He loves you. Let's thank Him for taking the punishment for what you did."

So Mother and Carol bowed their heads and thanked God for Jesus and His love.

Questions:

1. What did Carol do that was bad?
2. Did her mother spank her?
3. Did God hurt Carol for being bad?
4. Who was hurt instead of Carol?

A prayer:

Father above, thank You so much for Jesus. And thank You, Jesus, for coming down from heaven and dying for me. This I pray in Jesus' name. Amen.

A Bible thought:

God loves you so much that He punished Jesus instead of you for the bad things you do (John 3:16).

Bible reading: Isaiah 53:1-6

6

Don't Fight!

It is very easy to make people angry and sad. All you have to do is say, "You did too," if they say they didn't. Or you can call them names, and then probably they will call you something you don't like, and then there will be a big quarrel. Or you can tease your little brother and sister or play with the toys and other things when they don't want you to. You can almost always make them cry and yell by doing this.

But that is not the way a Christian boy or girl should act. Should a Christian try to make people angry and make them cry? No, of course not. A Christian should try to make people happy instead of angry and sad. It is easy to make people cry, but God wants us to make them glad.

The girl in this picture is whispering in her brother's ear. She is telling him a secret. She is saying that the boy and girl who live across the street are nice. Now this girl and her brother will go over and play and have lots of fun with the children across the street.

Jesus likes us to say good things about other people whenever we can, because then people will know that we are friends of His.

People will think, "Well, if Jesus' friends are nice, then Jesus must be best of all."

A Story

Once there was a man named Isaac. Isaac had many sheep. It was a hot day and the sheep were thirsty. They wanted to drink some water, but there wasn't any. So Isaac and his friends dug a deep hole in the ground, called a well. They found water down in the bottom of the hole and tied a bucket to a rope to get the water out, so the sheep could drink the water.

But some men came along and said to Isaac's friends, "Go away! This is our water."

"No," said Isaac's men. "We dug this well, and it is ours."

The men were going to hit each other and fight about it. Then Isaac came along and said, "No, don't fight. Let those men have the well, and we will go away and dig another one." So that is what they did. Isaac and his friends and his sheep went away. They wouldn't quarrel and fight, because they knew God didn't want them to. This is a true story that is in the Bible.

Questions:

1. Did Isaac let his men fight about the well?
2. Should a friend of Jesus try to make other people cry?
3. Can you think of some way to make another child happy? How would you do it?

A prayer:

Dear Father in heaven, please help me to be kind to other people and to help them and not to quarrel with them or make them sad. And thank You for helping Isaac. In Jesus' name. Amen.

A Bible thought:

It is good to make peace (Matthew 5:9).

Bible Reading: Genesis 26:17-22

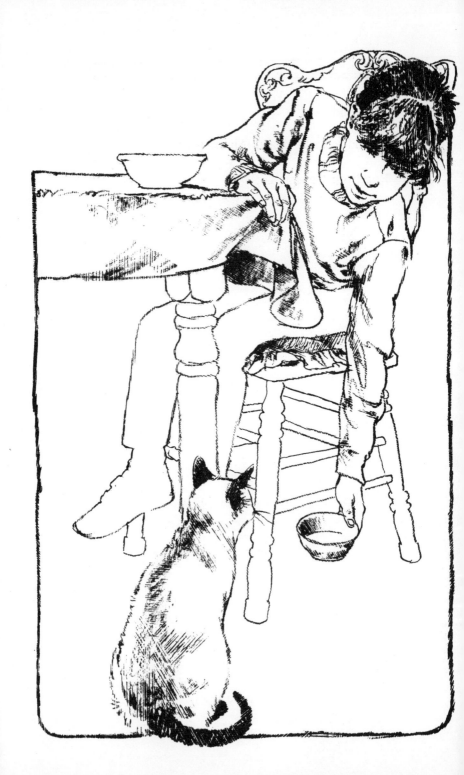

7

Helping Things That Are Hurt

This little girl is being kind to her kitty. It was hungry. The kitty saw the little girl eating her breakfast, so it was mewing. Now the little girl is feeding it.

We are glad the girl is being kind to the kitten. God likes this. He says in the Bible that He will give good things to people who are kind. You see, God up in heaven is watching everything that happens down here on earth. He knows all the birds and the animals, every one of them. He knows whenever one of them gets sick or hurt, and He knows when the kitties are hungry. So God knows about it whenever some boy or girl is kind to one of these birds or animals that He has made. God is glad when children are kind. When we are kind, it shows that we are trying to do what God wants. God is merciful and kind. So when we are kind, it shows that we have God helping us.

We can be kind to people too, and not just to kitties or birds. Can you think of some people you can be kind to? What could you do for them that would be nice and kind?

God says He will be kind to you if you are kind and nice to the things He has made.

A Story

There is a story in the Bible about a man who was going on a trip. He was walking along the road when some robbers jumped on him and took away all his money and knocked him down and hurt him. Then they ran away from him. The man couldn't get up because he was so badly hurt. Then another man came along, and the man who was hurt was very glad because now someone could help him. But the man who came along the road didn't stop. He looked at the hurt man but walked on without helping him at all. Another man passed by, but he did not stop.

Then the third man came along. He stopped and helped the man who was lying there. He put bandages and medicine on his hurt places and took him to a place to rest. He was kind and merciful to the man who was hurt. God liked this. Jesus told the people about this good man and said we should do things like that too.

Questions:

1. Was the good man merciful and kind when he helped the man who was hurt?
2. Does God like us to be merciful?
3. Have you ever been merciful by helping something or someone who was hurt or sick?

A prayer:

Father, we are often selfish and are kind to ourselves instead of to other people. Please help us to be kind to others and to try to help them so that You will be glad. In Jesus' name. Amen.

A Bible thought:

God says, Happy are those who are kind; I will be kind to them too (Matthew 5:7).

Bible Reading: Luke 10:30-37

8

Pure in Heart

This is a picture of a little girl who loves Jesus very much. She tries to do whatever He says. One thing God tells her to do is to always obey her father and mother, and she tries to do this.

Another thing God says is to pray. So she prays every night before she goes to sleep, and she prays sometimes during the day too. She can pray and thank God for many things while she is walking along. She likes to think about Jesus while she is walking along and about how much Jesus loves her. Sometimes when she is playing, she stops and thinks about these things. And it makes her very glad.

God loves this little girl. She thinks about God, and that pleases Him.

A Story

There is a wonderful story in the Bible about a woman named Ruth. We don't know very much about her when she was a little girl, except that she was born in a country far away where the people didn't know about God.

But when she grew up, one of God's men who was visiting near her house asked her to be his wife. She married this man and that is the way she learned about our heavenly Father. She loved God very much after she knew about Him. When her husband died, she and his mother went to live in another country far away. It took many days to get there, and they had to walk all the way. Ruth was willing to leave her own mother and father and go to the country where everyone loved our God. She was kind and sweet and good. She always wanted to do whatever God said. God liked this and gave her a new home with a dear little baby to love and play with. She trusted God, and God made her very happy.

Questions:

1. Why do you like Ruth?
2. Did Ruth love God?
3. Did God help Ruth?

A prayer:

Dear Father, thank You for Ruth who loved You so much. Help me to be like Ruth and to love You and trust You always. In Jesus' name. Amen.

A Bible thought:

God will be a special Friend of those who love Him best (Matthew 5:8).

Bible Reading: Ruth 1:16-18

9

Being Punished

Being punished isn't fun! No, it isn't at all! It hurts to be spanked, and it makes us sorry when we are scolded.

Should children be punished when they do wrong things, or would it be better to just let them go ahead and be bad? What would happen if children were never punished?

Those children would become worse and worse. If they did something wrong and weren't punished for it, they would do that wrong thing again and again. Soon they would decide to do something even worse. And since nobody punished them, they would never try to stop doing wrong things.

Then it might be necessary for an officer to come and take a child like that away from his home and put him with other children who are bad. He would take them to a special home for children whose parents haven't punished them for doing wrong things.

Then how sorry the father and mother would be! And how sorry the children would be! How much better it is to be punished when we do wrong things, so that we will remember not to do them again!

Why do we do bad things? It is because we have sin in our hearts, and Satan keeps trying to get us to do things that God says we must not do.

When we have been bad, what should we do about it? We must tell Jesus we are sorry and ask Him to forgive us. And we should tell Father or Mother. Sometimes that is hard to do, but it is important for us to learn to tell others that we have been wrong.

And never forget that if Jesus is our Savior, He will help us do good things—if we ask Him to.

A Story

Judy was hiding behind the sofa. She didn't want to wash the dishes, so she was hiding.

"Judy," Mother called. "Please come right away and help me with the dishes."

But Judy just stayed where she was and didn't say anything.

"Judy," Mother called again. Then she came in to see why Judy didn't come. "Judy," Mother said, "I think you are behind the sofa. Please come out right now, or I will have to punish you. Come now or you can't have any cookies to eat this afternoon."

Judy did not come.

But after a while Judy got tired of staying behind the sofa. She came out and helped her mother do the dishes. Afterward she said, "Now can I have some cookies, Mother, because I helped with the dishes?"

"No," Mother said, "not today. You know what I told you. No cookies today because you didn't come when I asked you to."

Judy cried and cried, but she didn't get any cookies. And the next day, when Mother called her to help with the dishes, she didn't want to miss any cookies. So can you guess what she did when she heard her mother calling? She came right away!

I would too. Wouldn't you?

Questions:

1. Where was Judy hiding?
2. Why was she hiding there?
3. What happened because she didn't come?
4. Do you think Judy comes now when her mother calls her?

A prayer:

Dear Father in heaven, You know when I've been bad, and I am sorry that I've done things I shouldn't. Thank You for Jesus, who died for my sins. Thank You for Daddy and Mother who help us to be good. In Jesus' name. Amen.

A Bible thought:

Children, obey your fathers and mothers (Ephesians 6:1).

Bible Reading: Hebrews 12:5-7, 11

10

There Is Only One God

The First Commandment: *Thou shalt have no other gods before me* (Exodus 20:3).

Did you ever have a puppy to play with? Was it warm and nice and wriggly?

Sometimes puppies get lost. Somebody comes walking along and the puppy follows him, and then what will happen? Pretty soon the puppy wants to come home again, but he doesn't know where. So you have to go and find him. And you say, "Now, puppy, stay home. Don't follow other people. You stay home with me, or I will spank you, because I don't want you to get lost."

God loves you more than you love your puppy, so God says, "Don't run away from Me. Don't pray to anyone else." There is only one God. You must not believe it if anyone says there are others. Only our God can hear us when we pray. Only He will love you every day.

In this picture you can see some people who have made a god with their hammers and axes, and now they are going to get down on their knees and pray to it. What a strange thing to do!

That is not a god. It is just something they made. And yet they think it can hear them and do things for them.

God does not like this. God does not want people to pray to foolish things. He wants them to pray only to Him.

A Story

Chung Lee is a little boy who lives in another country far away. One day Chung Lee's daddy said to him, "Come, Chung Lee. We must go and buy ourselves a god so that we can pray to him."

"Yes, Father," Chung Lee said. "I will go with you."

Chung Lee and his father went to the store. It was a store that had many kinds of little dolls in it. Some of them were pretty, and some of them were very ugly. Some of them had several arms and several heads. Chung Lee's father bought one that had lots of arms on it. They took it home and put it on a shelf in their house.

"Now," said Chung Lee's father, "let us call the family, and we will bow down and worship our new god. Perhaps he will give us food and help us."

So that is what Chung Lee's family did. Do you think this was good?

Questions:

1. Where is God?
2. Can God hear us when we talk to Him?
3. Can God see whatever we do?
4. Does God like it when people pray to dolls?

A prayer:

Thank You, O God, our heavenly Father, that we can pray to You and that You like us to come and talk to You in this way. Help us never to pray to anyone else, and help children like Chung Lee to hear about You so that they won't worship a doll anymore. In Jesus' name. Amen.

A Bible thought:

We must love God very, very much (Matthew 22:37).

Bible Reading: Isaiah 40:28-31

11

Never Pray to Anyone But God

The Second Commandment: *Thou shalt not make unto thee any graven image. Thou shalt not bow down thyself to them, nor serve them* (Exodus 20:4).

Here in this picture you can see a little girl holding a doll she has made. It isn't really a doll to play with, though, because she says it is her god, or idol. She prays to it and thinks it can hear her.

Do you think our true God is happy about this? Do you think He likes people to say He looks like this thing that the little girl has made? No, God does not like this at all. God is great and beautiful. We cannot hold Him in our hands, because He is up in heaven. It is not good for the little girl to think that God is like this bad-looking idol.

This little girl doesn't know that God is in heaven and that He loves her. She doesn't know that God made her and that God made everything. Why doesn't the little girl know about God? It is because someone has forgotten to tell her. Will you go and tell children like this little girl about our only true God?

A Story

Pretty Blossom is the name of a little child far away in another country. She was playing in the street one day when a friend came running up to her.

Her friend said, "Pretty Blossom. I have just heard something very nice. I want to tell you what I heard. I heard about a Man named Jesus. He is God's Son and lives up in heaven. He loves us and wants us to love Him."

Pretty Blossom was very glad to hear this good news. No one had ever told her this before. She went with her friend to a Good News Club where many other boys and girls were sitting and listening to a lady tell them about Jesus. Pretty Blossom was very happy. She went home and threw away the bad god she had made. After that she prayed to the true God in heaven and not to a bad-looking idol. Aren't you glad that Pretty Blossom's friends told her about Jesus?

Questions:

1. Where is the idol in this picture?
2. Should we pray to idols?
3. What did Pretty Blossom do with her idol?

A prayer:

Dear Father, thank You for being our only true God, who hears us up in heaven when we pray. Help me never to pray to any other god, for there is none other—only You. In Jesus' name. Amen.

A Bible thought:

Never pray to idols; only pray to God (Exodus 20:4-5).

Bible Reading: 1 John 5:20-21

12

No Swearing

The Third Commandment: *Thou shalt not take the name of the Lord thy God in vain* (Exodus 20:7).

"You're bad," Billy told his friend Jimmy. "I don't like you. I hope God kills you."

But Billy didn't mean that at all. He was angry at Jimmy. That is why he said that he wanted God to hurt Jimmy.

But God didn't like it at all when Billy said this. Billy was saying something that makes God angry. Billy was playing with God's great, wonderful name just as though it was a name like yours and mine. But God's name is different. The Bible tells us that His name is so great that someday when God's name is said, everybody will fall down. They will do this because they will be so afraid of God and His name. So you see, God's name is not something to play with or to say when we are angry. If we do, then God will punish us.

But if we love God, then we can call Him by His wonderful name when we pray. And He will listen to us and help us. We should thank God every day for telling us His name so that we can talk to Him.

So now do you see why Billy should never, never say God's name except in ways God likes? Yes, we must be very careful about this because we want to please God and make Him glad.

What should we do if we have made God angry by saying His name in ways we shouldn't? He is very kind to those who tell Him they are sorry. He can forgive us because Jesus died for our sins. How kind God is!

A Story

Some children were talking nicely about God. One of them said, "I love God the very best of all." The other one said, "I love Jesus best." A little girl who was listening said, "I love the Lord." Then the first boy said, "But Jesus is God, isn't He? I think Jesus and God and the Lord are different names God has."

Then the second little boy said, "I think that is right. Which one of His names do you like best?"

And the little girl said, "They are all God's names, and I like all of them best!"

Questions:

1. Is it right for people to say God's name when they are angry at each other?
2. What are some of God's names?
3. Which of His names do you like best?

A prayer:

Dear God, our Father in heaven, we are so glad that You are God and that Your name is so very great. Help us to be careful to say Your name in good ways and never in bad ways. We ask this in Jesus' wonderful name. Amen.

A Bible thought:

You must not say God's name in bad ways (Exodus 20:7).

Bible Reading: Revelation 22:1-7

13

Sunday Is Different

The Fourth Commandment: *Remember the sabbath day, to keep it holy* (Exodus 20:8).

Have you ever had a birthday? Yes, of course you have. Did you have a party on your birthday, and did you get some presents?

Yes, birthdays are very special days that children love to have.

Did you know that all of us have another special day too? It is a special day that comes every week. Every Sunday is a special day to remember what God has done for us.

After God had made the ground, the trees, the grass, and everything else, He made a special day of rest. All that day He rested. And God says that we should rest one day every week and not work like we do on other days. We call our rest day Sunday or the Lord's Day. It is God's special day that He has given us.

On Sunday you can go to God's house and learn more about Jesus. And on Sunday afternoon perhaps Mother or Daddy can read good books to you or you can go for a walk with them. Sunday is God's special day. It is the day our Lord Jesus became alive again after He had died for our sins. He wants you to love His day because He loves it too.

When we rest on Sunday, we can do better work for God on the other days of the week. But Sunday is not a day just to have fun. It is a day when we can be quieter than usual and learn more about our heavenly Father.

A Story

Mr. Grubbs came over to see Susan's father. Susan heard them talking about going away to a lake where they could have fun trying to catch some fish.

Mr. Grubbs said, "Boy, will we have fun! I hear the fish are really big there this year. Let's go over next Sunday and see how many we can get."

Susan thought of eating the nice fish her daddy would catch! She could almost taste how good they would be after Mother had cooked them.

But Susan was glad when her father said, "No, not Sunday. Susan and I go to Sunday school and church on Sunday. Let's go on Saturday afternoon instead."

So that is what they did. They didn't go on the Lord's Day, but they went on Saturday. Susan got to go with them, and she caught a fish too!

Questions:

1. What special day comes every week?
2. Did God make everything nice?
3. Is God glad on Sundays?
4. What are some special things to do on Sundays?

A prayer:

Our Father in heaven, thank You for giving us Sunday as Your special day. Thank You that it is different from other days and that we can rest from all our work and be glad. Then You are glad too. In Jesus' name. Amen.

A Bible thought:

Don't forget God's special day that comes every week (Exodus 20:8).

Bible Reading: Exodus 20:8-11

14

Doing What Mother and Father Say

The Fifth Commandment: *Honor thy father and thy mother* (Exodus 20:12).

Do you see how happy these boys and girls are? They are having fun. Mother asked them to rake up the leaves that had fallen on the grass in the yard. Are they crying because Mother asked them to help her? No, they are laughing. They want to help their mother and father and do whatever they say. They are being good and making God glad. God likes them to do whatever Mother asks them to. God is happy, their mother and father are happy, and the children are happy. So everybody is glad because they are doing what Mother asked them to do.

God wants us to love our mothers and fathers and help them. He likes us to wash the dishes and pick up our toys and put them away.

When you get bigger, God wants you to take care of Mother and Daddy. They can take care of you now when you are little. But someday when you are all grown up, you will need to help them even more than you do now. You will need to take care of them. And do you know something nice? God says He will give a special present to children who take care of their mothers and fathers. Would you like one of those nice presents?

A Story

Janet's big brother Bill was talking to Mother and Father.

"But, Dad," he said, "you ought to sell our old car. It's too old. Everybody else has a new car, and we should too."

"No," said Dad. "We don't need one. Ours works fine. We'll keep it for a while."

When Father had gone out, big brother began to act mad. He told Janet they needed a new car. "I guess Dad doesn't love us," Bill told his little sister, "because he doesn't get a new car that we can ride around in and see how surprised everybody is."

Little sister Janet didn't like what Bill was saying. "You shouldn't say things like that about Daddy," she said. Then Janet thought of a Bible verse she had learned in Sunday school. It said that children should listen to what their fathers and mothers say, and respect them. Janet said the verse to Bill. Bill looked surprised and didn't say anything.

But after a while he went out to see his dad. "I'm going to wash the car, Dad," he said. "It's a good car, and we want to keep it looking nice."

So you can see that Janet's Bible verse helped big brother Bill.

Questions:

1. How loud should you cry when Mother asks you to help her?
2. Why are the children in the picture happy?
3. Is God glad when His children help other people?
4. What can you do now to help?

A prayer:

O most holy God in heaven, help me always to make You glad by obeying my father and my mother, just as our Lord Jesus honored Mary and Joseph. This I ask in Jesus' name. Amen.

A Bible thought:

Honor your father and mother, and I will give you a long, good life (Exodus 20:12).

Bible Reading: Ephesians 6:1-4

15

Life Is Precious

The Sixth Commandment: *Thou shalt not kill* (Exodus 20:13).

Sometimes cats catch baby birds or mice and eat them. The cats kill the little birds, and we don't like them to do this.

God tells us in the Bible not to kill. Does this mean not to kill mice? No, it isn't talking about mice or birds. God says never to hurt other boys and girls or make them die. We must never hate other people and want to kill them.

Sometimes boys and girls like to play games where they just pretend they are shooting other people and killing them. I wonder if God likes this? Do you think God wants us to play like we don't care about what He says is wrong? He certainly does not.

Another thing God tells us is that we should like people and not want to hurt and kill them. If we don't like them we are being bad. God wants us to love them. That is the way for us to make God glad.

A Story

A boy named Jack was talking to his sister Ellen. They were talking about the girl who lived across the street. Her name was Mary.

"I don't like Mary at all," Ellen said. "She always breaks my dolls. I hate her!"

"Then you are worse than she is," Jack said. "It's bad to be mad at Mary, even if she does break your dolls."

"It isn't either," Jack's sister said. "If people hurt you, then you should hurt them."

"Oh, no!" Jack told his sister. "It isn't that way at all! We're supposed to be nice to everybody and try to help them, even if they hurt us."

"Even if they break our dolls?" Ellen asked.

"Yes," Jack said, "because that's what Jesus says."

And Jack was right. Jesus wants us always to be kind to other people and not be mad at them and want to hurt them.

Questions:

1. Does God want us to hurt people?
2. Why was Ellen mad at Mary?
3. What did Jack tell his sister?

A prayer:

Lord Jesus, please help us to love people and help them love You. Thank You for loving us even when we are bad. Help us to love other people even if they are bad. And help them to love You. We ask this in Jesus' name. Amen.

A Bible thought:

Be nice to people who try to hurt you, and don't try to get even with them (Matthew 5:44).

Bible Reading: Matthew 5:44-48

16

Boys and Girls

The Seventh Commandment: *Thou shalt not commit adultery* Exodus 20:14).

If you see a child walking along the street ahead of you, can you tell whether it is a boy or girl? Sure you can. It's usually easy, isn't it? Girls' hair often is longer and combed nicer than boys. Sometimes girls wear braids, and boys never do. Boys and girls wear different kinds of clothes, too.

And their bodies are made differently. Boys are stronger, and they are made that way so they can take care of their mothers and sisters. Girls aren't as strong as boys, because God made their bodies in such a wonderful way that someday they can get married and be mothers and have little babies. Boys aren't made that way at all. Boys could never be mothers. But someday, when they grow up, they can find the person God wants them to marry, and then they can be fathers.

God has given us rules about how boys and girls should act when they are together. Boys are to be kind and helpful to girls and see that nothing hurts them. Sometimes boys and girls have different gangs and pretend that they don't like each other. But when they are older, they will want to be with each other a lot.

Then they will need to know another of God's rules. Perhaps you will laugh when I tell you this, but they will want to hug and kiss each other. God says no. It is all right for them to do this after God has given them to each other and they are married, but not until then. That is why boys and girls should know God's seventh commandment, which says, "Thou shalt not commit adultery." This means that people who are married should love only the person God has given them to be a husband or wife. They should love no one else in the same way.

It also means that the Lord Jesus wants boys and girls to be strong and pure. They must not think wrong thoughts. Kissing and hugging each other before it is God's time often leads to wrong thoughts. So it is a good idea to decide now that you will never do anything that will make God sorry. That is why kissing games and dancing are not good for Christian boys and girls. If they aren't good for us, and God doesn't like things like that, then we will just not do them!

A Story

"Stop that!" yelled Jack, as he ran across the yard. "You leave Vicki alone!" Jack ran over to where John and Vicki were.

"Aw, I'm not hurting her," John said. Then he pushed Vicki again and almost made her fall down. Vicki was crying.

"Quit doing that right now!" Jack said as he ran up to them, all out of breath.

"You think you can make me stop?" John asked. "I guess I can push her if I want to. She's my sister."

"Oh, no, you can't," said Jack. "Not when I'm around. You may be bigger than I am, but you're a baby if you don't know you're not supposed to treat girls like that. You're supposed to be nice to them and help them, because that's what God says."

John started pushing Vicki again, so Jack grabbed him and pulled him away. John decided to run away. He went around the house and hid behind a bush. While John was hiding, he thought about what Jack had said. Jack said that God didn't want him to act that way.

"I guess Jack is right," John said to himself. "I guess I won't do that anymore." After that John tried to help Vicki instead of hurting her.

Questions:

1. Should boys try to help girls or tease them?
2. What did Jack tell John to stop doing?
3. What did John decide not to do anymore? Why?

A prayer:

Dear Father, thank You for sisters and brothers, and thank You for making both girls and boys. Bless now the child I will someday marry. Help us to wait for Your time. Amen.

A Bible thought:

People who are married must not want to marry someone else (Matthew 5:28).

Bible Reading: Genesis 24:53-61

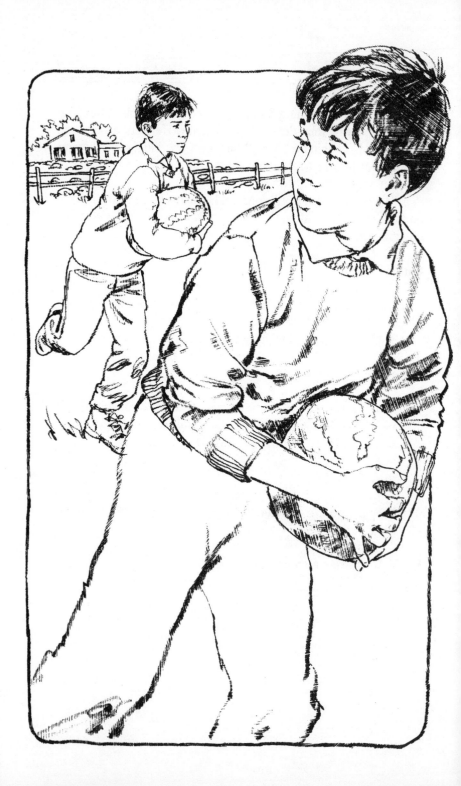

17

Don't Take It

The Eighth Commandment: *Thou shalt not steal* (Exodus 20:15).

These boys in the picture are taking watermelons that don't belong to them. They are stealing them from the man who owns them. And that is bad. These are big boys, and they should know it is wrong to steal. Even little children know that stealing is wrong. God says in the Bible that you should never take anything that doesn't belong to you.

Why does God say this? Well, would you like some boy to come along and sneak away with some of your toys and then say they are his? No, you wouldn't like that at all. And God doesn't like it either. It's against His laws, and He knows what is good and bad.

Have you ever stolen anything? If you have, do you know what to do? You should take back what you have stolen and give it to the person it belongs to. And then you should tell Mother or Daddy, and they will help you tell God about it and ask Him to forgive you.

A Story

Elena looked at the big doll sitting there on the chair. Elena wished and wished she had such a big doll. But it wasn't hers. She was playing at Jessie Mae's house, and the big doll belonged to Jessie Mae.

Elena wanted it so much that she decided to steal it. When no one was looking, she ran out of the house with it and took it home with her, just as fast as she could go. She hurried into her own house with the big doll in her arms and hid it behind the sofa where she had some other important things. Then she got some bread and butter and jam and sat down to eat it and think about her big new doll.

"Oh, boy!" she said to herself. "It's mine now. I'm going to play with the big doll every day all the rest of my life!"

But Elena didn't really feel very happy about it. The more she thought about it, the worse she felt. "God doesn't like this," she thought. "I'd better take the doll back to Jessie Mae."

So she did.

Jessie Mae said, "Oh, were you playing outside with my big doll? That's nice. Let's play some more with her in here."

That night when Elena was going to bed, she felt very happy. "Thank You, Lord," she said, "for helping me to take the big doll back."

Some questions:

1. Whom did the big doll belong to?
2. Who stole the doll?
3. Where is the doll now?
4. Is Elena glad or sorry that she took the doll back to its own house?

A prayer:

Dear Lord Jesus, help me to always love You and always do what is right. Help me not to steal anything ever, even if I want it very much. And if I have stolen something, help me to take it back. Thank You for helping me. In Your name. Amen.

A Bible thought:

If you have stolen something, take it back and never do it again (Ephesians 4:28).

Bible Reading: Luke 6:20-21

18

Telling the Truth

The Ninth Commandment: *Thou shalt not bear false witness* (Exodus 20:16).

The boy in the picture is telling his friend about the fish that he caught. He is showing how big it was. He says that it was so big that he could hardly lift it. I wonder if this boy is telling the truth. I think maybe he is telling a lie and trying to get the other boy to think that the fish was big when really it wasn't that big at all.

What do you think about this? Is it all right to tell lies? No, God hates lies. He loves to have us tell the truth.

It is easy for us to tell lies like this boy and to say things that aren't true, but God says never to do this. He wants us always to tell things right. If you do something naughty and somebody asks if you did it, you should say yes. Perhaps you will be punished, but you will be pleasing God. That is more important than anything else.

Do you know who tries to get us to tell lies? It is Satan. He is glad when he gets some boy or girl to obey him and tell a lie.

The Lord Jesus is true and pure. He tells no lie. He can make

Satan stay away from us if we ask Him to. God is glad when His children say things that are right. Do you make God happy because you tell the truth?

A Story

Benny and Gordon were brothers. These two brothers liked bread and butter with lots of jam on it. Sometimes their mother let them have some in the afternoons, and sometimes she said no. One afternoon when Benny and Gordon had been playing outside a long time, they came into the kitchen as hungry as bears.

"Mother, may we have some bread and butter and jam?" they asked.

"Not this time," Mother said, "because it is almost suppertime."

But when Mother went upstairs to put on a clean dress for supper, the boys quickly got out the bread and butter and jam, and ate some of it. When they heard their mother coming downstairs, they quickly ate their last bite and started to play with some toys.

Mother took one look at Benny's face. There was jam on it. "Did you boys take some bread when I told you not to?" she asked.

"No," said Benny, "we didn't." But Benny forgot about the jam! So mother sent him to bed without any supper.

Gordon looked in the mirror. He didn't have any jam on his face.

"Did you take some too?" Mother asked him.

Gordon thought about what to say. If he told the truth, he knew what Mother would do. If he told a lie, he knew God wouldn't like that. Can you guess what he finally said?

Questions:

1. Who always knows whether we are telling the truth or not?
2. How did Benny's mother know he was telling a lie?
3. Is it all right to tell little lies?

A prayer:

Father in heaven, help me to tell the truth always and not tell lies. May everyone know that I belong to You. In Jesus' name. Amen.

A Bible thought:

Never tell lies (Exodus 20:16).

Bible Reading: Philippians 4:8-9

19

Wanting Other People's Things

The Tenth Commandment: *Thou shalt not covet* (Exodus 20:17).

This girl in the picture wishes she could catch a nice fish like her brother did. Do you see his fish? The girl doesn't have any yet. She is sorry, and I think maybe she is going to cry about it.

But will it help her catch fish if she begins to cry? No, of course not. And do you know that God doesn't want her to cry about it or feel sorry? God wants her to be glad that her brother has caught a nice fish, instead of being sorry. God tells us in the Bible that it is bad to want other people's things.

Why is it bad to want another child's toys? Because then you are really scolding God for not giving you the toys. God knows what is best for you. If he doesn't want you to have a toy like another child's, then you should be happy without it and play with something else. God is always good, and God knows best. That is why we should be happy with whatever He gives us and thank Him and not want a lot of other things instead.

A Story

I want to tell you about a little boy called Gimmy. That wasn't his real name, though. His real name was Jimmy, but people called him Gimmy because he always wanted other people's things and kept saying, "Gimmy this," or, "Gimmy that!"

One day Gimmy's father gave him a tricycle for his birthday. He took it outside to ride. While he was riding down the sidewalk, he saw his friend Alan playing with a hammer his father had given to him.

"Gimmy that hammer," Gimmy said. But Alan wouldn't. So Gimmy cried and cried about it until his father came out to see what the trouble was.

"Alan won't give me his hammer," Gimmy said.

"But you have your tricyle," said Father. "Why don't you play with it?"

"I don't want a tricycle. I want a hammer!" Gimmy said. So Gimmy's father took away the tricycle and gave him a hammer.

Pretty soon Gimmy was crying again. "I don't want this old hammer," he said. "Gimmy a truck. That's what I want."

Poor Gimmy. He had never learned to be happy with the things he had.

Questions:

1. Why was Jimmy called Gimmy?
2. Did he want a tricycle or a hammer or a truck?
3. Does Jesus want us to be happy with the things He gives us?

A prayer:

O Lord Jesus, help me to be glad and not complain. Help me to know how great and kind You are, and help me not to want what belongs to other people. This I ask in Your name. Amen.

A Bible thought:

Be happy with what you have (Hebrews 13:5).

Bible Reading: Psalm 23:1-6

20

Going to Sunday School

Do you see what is happening in this picture? Two girls are going to Sunday school. Can you see the church waiting for them to come in? But now I will tell you a secret that the picture won't tell. The secret is that one of these girls has never been to Sunday school in her whole life. Her mother and father don't know Jesus, and so they never take her to Sunday school. But yesterday the other girl asked her to come with her, and now they are almost there. Do you think she is going to have a good time at Sunday school, learning about Jesus?

A Story

"This is it," Daddy said, as he stopped the car.

Ellen looked at the big new house. It was the new house that Daddy had bought, and today was the day to begin living in it. Ellen ran all around the house and liked everything she saw. Then she ran all through the house and stopped in every room.

"I like this house, Daddy," she said, when she came back.

That afternoon the little girl from next door came over to play. Her name was Nancy.

"Can you go with me to Sunday school tomorrow?" Nancy asked.

"Oh, I'd like to," Ellen said, "but I've never been to Sunday school. Let's go and ask my mother."

Mother said she could, so that is how Ellen got a new house and a new friend and a new Sunday school, all at the same time.

Questions:

1. Do you think God is glad because the girl next door asked Ellen to come to Sunday school with her?
2. Do you know anyone who doesn't go to Sunday school?
3. Would you like to ask him or her to come with you next Sunday?

A prayer:

Dear Father in heaven, there are so many children who never go to Sunday school and don't know about You. Please help me to get other children to come and hear about Your love for them. In Jesus' name. Amen.

A Bible thought:

Jesus said, Please go and tell other people how much I love them (Mark 16:15).

Bible Reading: Luke 6:6-11

21

Who Should Go to Church?

Some people think that Sunday school is only for children, and church is only for fathers and mothers and older people. But that isn't true. Sunday school is for the whole family, and so is church. Christian children who don't go to church are disobeying the Lord. He tells us in the Bible that we should.

Why is it so important to go to church? One reason is that God has commanded it, and that is really all the reason we need. Another reason is that it reminds us of the Lord. When we read the Bible and pray by ourselves, it is good. But when we see others worshiping God, it helps us to worship and praise Him even more than before.

When we are in church, we must be careful to be quiet and listen to what the minister is saying. If there is a choir in our church, we should try to hear and understand the words that are being sung. When there is prayer, we should listen and say in our hearts the same words being said by the one praying out loud. During the sermon when the pastor or someone else is telling about what the Bible says, we should listen and not think about other things. We should think about what is being said. Perhaps we cannot understand it all, but if we listen we will understand some of it. Then we can pray quietly in our hearts and say thank you to God for giving us teachers and pastors to tell us what He wants us to know. We can thank God for the church.

A Story

"I'm not going to church today, Mother," Billy announced one Sunday morning.

"You're not?" Mother said. "Why not?"

"I want to play," Billy said, "and I can't understand what Pastor Burton is talking about in his sermon. I just don't want to go."

"Well, that's interesting," Mother said. "What does God want you to do?"

"I don't know," Billy said. "Does the Bible tell us?"

"Yes," Mother said, "it does. It says not to forget to go to church. God says you should go."

"Then I will," Billy said, "because I want to do whatever God says. But could I stay home today and start again next week?"

"That's dangerous," Mother said. "If you do it once, you will want to do it again. Better not do it at all."

"OK," Billy said. "Hurry up, Mom, or we'll be late."

Aren't you glad that Billy decided he should obey God?

Questions:

1. Is it all right for children to go to church?
2. Do you listen to the choir sing when you are in church?
3. How much noise should we make in church?

A prayer:

Our Father in heaven, thank You for church. Thank You that we can go there to pray together and listen to the pastor tell us more about You. In Jesus' name. Amen.

A Bible thought:

Don't forget about going to church; and help other people to remember it too (Hebrew 10:25).

Bible Reading: Psalm 122:1-4

22

It's Not Fun

All of us are sick sometimes. This means that our bodies are no longer working quite the way they should.

Sometimes the sickness is not very important, as when we get a little cold. In a few days it may go away.

Sometimes we have measles or chicken pox or mumps, and we must stay in bed several days.

And sometimes we might have rheumatic fever or some other disease that makes us stay in bed many weeks.

When you are sick, sometimes you don't want to do anything except lie quietly in bed and sleep. Since the doctor usually has told Mother and Father what is best for you, you should be careful to do just what they say. If you are supposed to stay in bed, then that is the best thing to do. Don't always be coaxing to get up. If you are supposed to eat just certain things, then don't beg for something else that might not be good for you to eat when you are sick.

After you feel better, then there are many interesting things for a sick child to do. You can color pictures, write letters, and read books. You can clip out pictures from magazines and paste them in scrapbooks, and listen to children's programs on the radio.

There is another thing you can do—something a Christian boy or girl can do no matter whether he is well or sick. You can pray. Sometimes when one is sick, he can do more for God than when he is well! Praying is more important than doing things. When we are sick, we can't do very much other work for Jesus. But we can pray for our friends and for missionaries far away. Perhaps that is the most important work that anyone can ever do.

And we can be happy and cheerful. That is important work too!

A Story

Linda was crying. "Oh, oh, oh!" she wailed. "My tummy hurts." Linda had been sick in bed all day, and she still felt bad all over.

"I'm sorry you aren't feeling well," Mother said, "but I think you will feel better in the morning."

And sure enough, when she woke up it was morning and she felt much better.

"Can I get up and play?" she asked her mother. But Linda really wasn't quite sure she wanted to get up, because she still felt tired.

"No, not today," Mother said, "but maybe tomorrow."

"But, Mother," Linda said, "I'll get too tired just being in bed all day."

"Oh," Mother said, "I think we can fix that. Let's think up some things to do."

Linda and Mother made a list. Linda told her mother what to write, and Mother took a pen and a piece of paper and wrote what Linda said. Here is the list:

Eat some breakfast
Listen to the radio
Sleep

Play with dolls
Pray for missionaries
Count cars going by outside
Play with kitty
Play with jigsaw puzzle
Pray for Daddy at work

After Linda and Mother had made the list, Linda felt tired and decided to take a nap. She slept all morning. Then after lunch she did some of the things on her list. Before very long it was dinnertime. Linda's daddy came home with a new toy for her, so Linda had a nice day being sick. The next morning she could get up because she was all well again.

Questions:

1. Have you ever been sick?
2. Was it fun?
3. What were some of the things to do on Linda's list?
4. Can you think of other things to do that Linda didn't put down on the list?

A prayer:

Lord, thank You for being with me when I am sick and when I am well. Help me to know always that You are near. I ask this in Jesus' name. Amen.

A Bible thought:

When you are sick or in trouble, God will be right there with you (see Psalm 120:1).

Bible Reading: Luke 18:35-43

23

Money for Jesus

This big girl is holding a bankbook in her hands. The book tells how much money she has downtown in the bank. She can go there and get her money whenever she wants it. The people at the bank will give her extra pennies too, because she lets them keep her money.

This girl's name is Susan. Whenever Susan gets any money, she gives part of it to God. She likes to take her money to Sunday school, and that is the way she gives it to God. She takes some to Sunday school and takes some downtown to the big bank.

All of our money, all of our clothes, and our houses belong to God. Everything we have belongs to Him. God lets us have these things to use, but they really belong to Him. Do you thank God for letting you use His things? God will tell us what to do with His money. He will tell us how much to take to Sunday school and how much to put in the bank and how much to use to buy candy and clothes and other things. God is kind to give us things and to help us.

A Story

One day Susan—remember, that is the name of this girl in the picture—made some good cookies and took them to some other houses and asked the people in the other houses if they would like to buy some of them. She said they could have them for 25¢. Many people wanted cookies, so Susan got about $2.00. She gave some of the money to her mother to pay for the flour and sugar and butter she used to make the cookies. Then she put some in an envelope to give to missionaries. Then she went to the bank and gave the rest to the people there to keep for her. They marked her bankbook to tell how much money she had given to them to keep for her. It is God's money, and she is glad.

Questions:

1. What is this girl's name?
2. What is she holding in her hand?
3. Why is she happy?
4. What did she do with the money she got from selling cookies to other people?

A prayer:

Dear God in heaven, thank You for giving me so many good things to use. They are all Yours, but You let me use them, and I am glad. Help me to be careful with all Your things and use them as You want me to. In Jesus' name. Amen.

A Bible thought:

It isn't good to want lots of money (1 Timothy 6:10).

Bible Reading: Mark 10:23-27

24

Do You Love God?

How much do you love God? Do you love Him just a little bit, or do you love Him very much? If we love God a lot, we will do what He tells us to do. Then we will be happy and glad. And then He will give us rewards for the good things we do.

But if we don't love God very much, then we won't even try to do what He wants us to. So you see, it makes a lot of difference whether you really love God or not. And God cares about it too. He wants you to love Him, and if you don't, it makes Him sad.

Would you like to love God more? You can! All you need to do is to ask God to help you love Him more. Then His Holy Spirit will fill you with so much love that you will have all you need.

Even a little child who has Jesus as His Savior may come to our heavenly Father and say, "Dear Father, I want to love *You* more and more. Please have the Holy Spirit help me love You more." And God will gladly do this wonderful thing and help you love Him.

A Story

"Do you love God?" a father asked his little boy.

"Yes," said the boy, "because He loves me so much and has given me so many nice things." And then he said, "Daddy, do you love God?"

"Yes, I do," his father said, "but I need to love Him more. Let's ask God to help us to love Him the way we should."

So the boy and his father both got down on their knees and asked God to help them. They did this every day, and do you know what? God was glad when they asked Him to help them, and God answered their prayers. Soon they felt more love for God than before, and other people noticed that they were becoming kinder and happier.

Would you like God to help you too? He will, just as He helped the boy and his father.

Questions:

1. How much do you love God?
2. Would you like to love God more?
3. Will God help us to love Him more if we ask Him?

A prayer:

Our Father in heaven, we do love You, and we want to love You more and more. Please help us. In Jesus' name. Amen.

A Bible thought:

We must love God very much (Luke 10:27).

Bible Reading: Psalm 42:1-5

25

Being a Helper

This little girl is giving her puppy a bath. I wonder if the puppy is glad? Most puppies don't like to take baths, so maybe this one wants to get out and run away.

But the puppy needs a bath, and so it is good for the little girl to give him one. She is working hard getting him all clean and pretty. She is washing the puppy's back.

The girl is being a good helper. Shall I tell you why? It is because she likes to help and because she likes to do whatever she is asked to do. She knows it is right to help and not just to do whatever she wants. She knows that Jesus says to do whatever our mothers and fathers tell us, even when we don't want to.

This little girl can wash dishes and dry them, but she can't put them away very well because she can't reach high enough. But she can put toys away and help keep the living room tidy.

Do you know any nice child at your house who can do all these things?

A Story

Sharon and Peter weren't very happy at all. In fact, they were crying loudly. Just then Daddy walked into the room where they were.

"What a terrible noise," he said, "and what funny-looking faces. Whatever is the trouble?"

"Boo hoo," cried Sharon and Peter. "Mother asked us to help her put the knives and forks and spoons on the table. Boo hoo, we don't want to."

"Why not?" Daddy asked. "We need them to eat dinner with, don't we?"

"Yes," Sharon and Peter said, "but we shouldn't have to put them on."

"Who should then?" Daddy wanted to know.

Sharon and Peter stopped crying and looked at each other. They couldn't think of anybody else to do it. Mother was busy getting dinner ready, and Daddy had just come home.

"I guess we should," they said.

"Then you'd better get it done."

Daddy looked like he wasn't pleased by the way they had been acting, so they ran into the kitchen and got to work fast!

Questions:

1. What do you think would have happened to Peter and Sharon if they had just kept on crying instead of doing their work?
2. When you are asked to help do something, do you say, "Sure, I'll help," or do you pout and cry?
3. What does Jesus like us to do?

A prayer:

Our Father, we need Your help to love other people as we should. Help us to love them and to help them, too. In Jesus' name we ask this. Amen.

A Bible thought:

Be kind to each other (Ephesians 4:32).

Bible Reading: Ephesians 6:1-8

26

The Lord's Table

Can you guess where these children are and what they are doing? They are in church, up near the front, looking at the Communion table. The table has plates full of little pieces of bread or special wafers, and little cups of wine or grape juice.

Have you seen a table like this one in your church? Yes, I think you have. The food on the table is there because Jesus wants His friends to eat it. Just before Jesus went away to die on the cross for us, He was eating with His friends. He told them to come together again often and eat in this special way.

God likes His children to do this. It is a time when we think about Jesus and His love. We remember that Jesus died for our sins and took them all away if we belong to Him. When Christians eat this bread and drink from the cup, they are doing what He told them to keep on doing until He comes again. So it is a time to be very glad that Jesus loves us and to be very sorry for bad things we have done.

How old should a child be before taking Communion, or the Lord's Supper? Different churches have different rules about this. First of all, a child should love Jesus and know that He has died for his sins. Only Christians who love Jesus may eat this bread and drink from these cups.

A Story

Marilyn Johnson was talking to her pastor. They were talking about Jesus and how much He loves children and their mothers and fathers. "Jesus died for me," Marilyn said, "so He must love me very much."

"Yes, He was punished for what you did," her pastor said.

Then Marilyn started to cry. "Yes," she said, "God hurt Jesus for what *I* did. Oh, I am so sorry for hurting Jesus, and I love Him so much. I want to do something to show Him how much I love Him."

Questions:

1. What could Marilyn do to show Jesus that she loves Him?
2. What could you do?
3. When will you do it?

A prayer:

O God, our heavenly Father, how great You are! We cannot begin to tell You how thankful we are for Jesus and His great love. Thank You that Jesus came to die for me. In Jesus' name. Amen.

A Bible thought:

We love Him because He loved us first (1 John 4:19).

Bible Reading: Matthew 26:26-29

27

What Is a Guest?

These people in the picture are very happy because some friends have come to visit them. They haven't seen each other for a long time, and now they can talk about things and enjoy being together again.

The people who have come to visit are called guests. Sometimes guests come just to dinner, and sometimes they stay all night and visit for several days.

It is fun when other boys and girls come to visit, because then we can let them play with our toys. It is good to help them have a nice time.

Do you know that God likes us to have guests and invite people to eat with us? Yes, that is what the Bible tells us. It says, "Don't forget to invite people to come and visit you."

Why does God like this? Because God loves to have us be friendly. He wants us to like other people and help them.

And one of the best ways to make them happy is to ask them to come and visit us.

We should be kind to people we don't know very well and not only to our good friends. So if some other children move into a house near you, it is nice to ask them to come and play with you even though you don't know them very well.

When guests are in your home, what are some ways to make them glad? One way is to be quiet and help your mother. Perhaps you can help set the table and afterward wash the dishes. It is interesting to talk to guests when your mother and dad are busy. It is fun to find out things about where they live and interesting things they have seen and done.

A Story

Mary Ann's mother was excited and happy, and Mary Ann was too, because it was the day that Aunt Mae and Uncle George were coming for a visit. Aunt Mae and Uncle George didn't have any children to play with. But Mary Ann was glad they were coming, because she knew they would talk and play with her. It was always fun when they came to visit.

As soon as their car drove up the driveway, Mary Ann ran outside and gave Uncle George and Aunt Mae a great big kiss. By that time, Mother and Daddy were there too, and everyone was talking at the same time. So Mary Ann went into the house and began to set the table for dinner. By the time Mother and Daddy and Aunt Mae and Uncle George came in, her job was almost done.

Mother said, "Oh, thank you, Mary Ann. Now we can sit right down and eat. Thank you for setting the table so nicely."

And Aunt Mae said, "I like to come here to visit, because everyone is so happy and helps so nicely."

Mary Ann was happy because she had helped make Aunt Mae and Uncle George glad.

Questions:

1. What did Mary Ann do when she heard the car?
2. What did Mary Ann do in the house?

3. Can you think of some guests you have had at your house? Who were they?
4. What are some ways to make guests happy?

A prayer:

Father, we bow our heads now to thank You for letting us have friends to come and visit us. Help us to love them and to do kind things for them and help us also to love people who are not our friends. In Jesus' name. Amen.

A Bible thought:

Don't forget to be kind to people you don't know (Hebrews 13:2).

Bible Reading: Genesis 18:1-8

28

What Is a Missionary?

Who is this woman in the picture? She is a woman who lives far away in another country. Her house looks different from yours, doesn't it? Can you see her little boy and little girl? The little boy and his sister have never heard about Jesus. No one has ever told them that Jesus loves them. Would you like to go and tell them? If you do, you will be a missionary. A missionary is someone who goes and tells people about Jesus.

If you go to tell them about Jesus, you won't be able to talk to them at first, because these people don't talk like we do. They have different words. We say "good-bye" when someone is going away, but these people say "adios." All their words are different, so you will need to go to school and learn their words so that you can talk to them about Jesus.

Do you know someone who is a missionary? Who is it? Maybe your mother or daddy can help you think of the name of a missionary you know.

Would you like to pray now for little girls and boys in other countries? Ask God to send someone to tell them about Jesus, so they will know Him too, just as you do.

A Story

"I'm going to be a missionary when I get big," Janice told her mother. "I'm going to get into an airplane and go far away and tell other people about Jesus."

"That's fine," her mother said. "But you don't have to wait until you grow up to be a missionary. You can be a missionary now."

"Oh, good," Janice said. "Tomorrow is Sunday, so can I get in an airplane and go far away tomorrow and be a missionary?"

"No," Mother said. "But you can get on your tricycle right now and go over to Jimmy Green's house and see if he can come to Sunday school with us tomorrow."

So Janice did. And Jim asked his mother if he could go to Sunday school with Janice, and his mother said yes.

Janice forgot about her tricycle and ran home as fast as she could. "Mother," she said, "Jimmy is going to go to Sunday school with me, so now am I a missionary?"

"Yes," Mother said, "you really are. You are a missionary to Jimmy now. And when you grow up, you can be a missionary in some other country far away."

Questions:

1. Was Janice a missionary? Why?
2. Did Janice have to get into an airplane and go to another country to be a missionary?
3. Would you like to be a missionary? Can you think of someone to invite to Sunday school as Janice did?

A prayer:

Our Father in heaven, help me to be a missionary and tell people about You. Help everybody to know that Jesus died for them. In Jesus' name we ask this. Amen.

A Bible thought:

Jesus said, Go everywhere and tell people about Me (Mark 16:15).

Bible Reading: Isaiah 52:7-10

29

It's Good for Families to Pray Together

Can you see what the people in this family are doing? Everyone has his eyes closed. They are praying. The father is talking out loud to God, and the mother and children are talking in their hearts so that only God can hear them. Only the father is talking now, but soon the mother will pray, and each child will pray too.

After this family has talked to God, they will read from the Bible. Sometimes each one takes a turn reading a verse. Daddy and Mother help the children who can't read. They say the words, and the children say them too.

Sometimes this family sings after they have read their Bible, and sometimes Father reads to them from a Bible storybook or from a book telling about missionaries. And then they talk about things that have happened that day. Sometimes they take turns and tell about things they are glad for or sorry about.

It is good for families to read the Bible together and to pray together and to talk together. God likes it when families do this.

A Story

LuAnne was visiting her friend Mary, who lived across the street. Mary's mother had asked her to stay for dinner, and Mother said she could. So of course LuAnne was very glad. After the meal was over, Mary's father said, "Now it's time for family prayers."

"What are family prayers?" LuAnne wanted to know.

"Come and find out," Mary said. The two little girls went into the living room with Mary's mother and father and two brothers, Jim and Carl. First Mary's father read to them from a big book of Bible stories. He read about Jesus making a sick girl well again. Then they took turns praying. When it was LuAnne's turn, she said, "Thank You, Jesus, for letting me come and listen to the Bible story."

After each one had prayed, they all sang, "Jesus loves me, this I know." LuAnne knew this song because she had learned it in Sunday school. That night, when LuAnne was home again and Father was tucking her into bed, she said, "Daddy, tomorrow let's have family prayers at our house too."

Her daddy thought that was a good idea. Now every night after dinner LuAnne and her mother and father and brother and sister read the Bible and pray together. Isn't that a good idea?

Questions:

1. What did LuAnne tell her father when he was tucking her into bed?
2. What are some things to do in family prayers?
3. Are family prayers good to have?

A prayer:

Dear Lord Jesus, thank You for loving all of us here in our family. Thank You that we can pray together and read the Bible. Help us to understand it and to do what it says. In Your Name. Amen.

A Bible thought:

If children learn to love the Lord at home, they will love Him all the rest of their lives (Proverbs 22:6).

Bible Reading: Deuteronomy 6:6-9

30

The Bible Is God's Book

There is a song that children sometimes sing that goes like this:

The B-I-B-L-E,
Yes, that's the Book for me;
I stand alone
On the Word of God,
The B-I-B-L-E.

The B-I-B-L-E,
Yes, that's the Book for me;
I read and pray
And then obey
The B-I-B-L-E.

Perhaps you know this song and have sung it many times in Sunday school. It is a good song because it talks about the Bible. Do you know what the Bible looks like? Do you have a Bible in your home? Yes, I am quite sure you do. But do you know who wrote the Bible? I want to tell you because this is very important. God wrote the Bible. It is His Book. And God wants us to read His Book so we will know what He is telling us.

The Bible is like a letter. It is God's letter to you and to me. It doesn't look like a letter because it is so big, but it tells just what God wants us to know.

The Bible is a letter from God to you and me, and He wants us to read it.

A Story

"Mother, did I get any letters from the mailman?" Bob asked.

"There is a letter for you on the table," Mother said. "Why don't you read it now?"

"I don't see any letter," Bob said. "Where is it? There is nothing on the table except my Bible."

"That's what I mean," Mother said. "That is your letter. It is a letter from God. Why don't you see what He says?"

"I guess I will," Bob said. "I guess God wants me to read His letter. Will you help me read it?"

"Surely," Mother said.

So Bob and Mother sat down and read some of God's letter. Would you like to read God's letter too?

Questions:

1. Who wrote the Bible?
2. Does God want us to read His letter?
3. If you can't read, how can you find out what the Bible says?

A prayer:

Lord Jesus, thank You for telling us so many wonderful things in the Bible. Help us to understand them and to do whatever You want us to. In Your name we ask these things. Amen.

A Bible thought:

God wrote everything that is in the Bible (2 Timothy 3:16).

Bible Reading: Nehemiah 8:1-3

Moody Press, a ministry of the Moody Bible Institute, is designed for education, evangelization, and edification. If we may assist you in knowing more about Christ and the Christian life, please write us without obligation: Moody Press, c/o MLM, Chicago, Illinois 60610.